# ZOOM!

## The Complete Paper Airplane Kit!

Written and illustrated by
## Margaret A. Hartelius

Cover illustration by
## Cameron Eagle

Text and interior illustrations copyright © 1991, 2003 by Margaret A. Hartelius.
Cover illustration copyright © 2003 by Cameron Eagle. All rights reserved.
Published by Grosset & Dunlap, a division of Penguin Young Readers Group,
345 Hudson Street, New York, NY, 10014. GROSSET & DUNLAP is a trademark of
Penguin Group (USA) Inc. Published simultaneously in Canada. Printed in the U.S.A.

ISBN 978-0-448-463174-1                    15 14 13 12 11 10 9 8

# Contents

Shorty

| | Page |
|---|---|
| Hints | 3 |
| Lazy Drifter | 4 |
| Plain Plane | 6 |
| Zoom-A-Room | 8 |
| E-Z Flyer | 10 |
| Dipper | 12 |
| Shorty | 14 |
| Dive Bomber | 16 |
| Super Looper | 18 |
| Smoothy | 20 |
| Little Bat | 22 |
| Fly-Any-Way | 24 |
| Shooting Star | 26 |
| Owl | 28 |
| Buzz Bug | 30 |
| Decorating Your Plane | 32 |

# *Hints*

1. Use the paper and stickers in this kit
   to make the paper airplanes in this book.
   When you finish the planes in the book,
   invent some of your own.

2. If you run out of paper, use notebook
   paper or typing paper. And if you run
   out of stickers, you can decorate your planes
   with crayons, colored pencils, or markers.

3. As you fold your planes, crease each fold sharply.
   Using your fingernail works well.

4. After you make a plane, launch it gently.
   Then try throwing it harder.
   See which way it flies best.

5. Try folding the wing tips up. Try folding them down.
   Put one wing tip up and one wing tip down.
   Does the plane fly better? Will it do loops?
   Or does it just go "clunk"?

6. To decorate a plane, you can put the
   stickers anywhere you want, unless
   the directions for that plane tell you
   where to place the stickers.

7. You can also use the stickers to keep
   the wings or the body together and
   to add extra weight to the plane.

8. Fly your planes outdoors when there
   is little or no wind. (If you fly them
   in a wind, they'll just blow away!)
   Most of the planes fly well indoors—
   just ask a grown-up if it's okay.

# Lazy Drifter

**1.**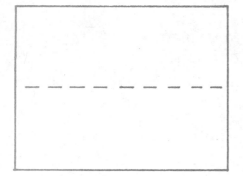

Fold the paper in half like this.

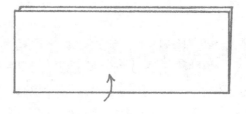

**2.**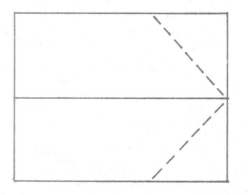

Open the paper flat again.

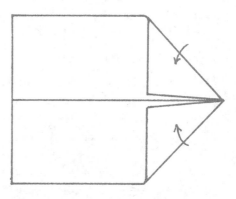

Fold down the corners to the center crease.

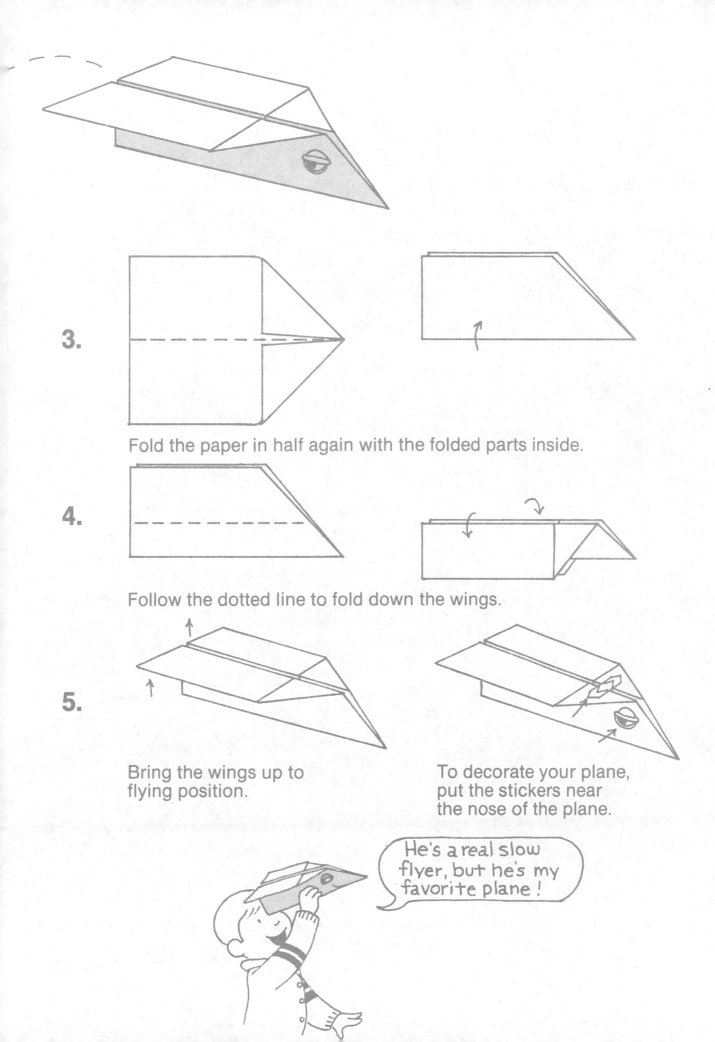

**3.** Fold the paper in half again with the folded parts inside.

**4.** Follow the dotted line to fold down the wings.

**5.** Bring the wings up to flying position.

To decorate your plane, put the stickers near the nose of the plane.

He's a real slow flyer, but he's my favorite plane!

# Plain Plane

**1.**

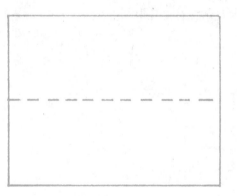

Fold the paper in half like this.

**2.**

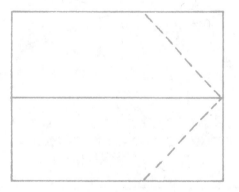

Open the paper flat again.

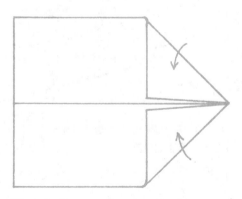

Fold down the corners to the center crease.

# (The Standard)

**3.**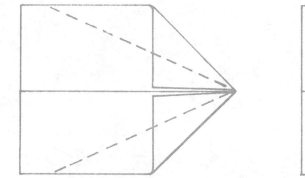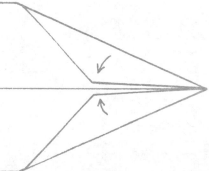

Fold down these corners to the center crease like this.

**4.**

Fold the plane in half
with the folded parts inside.

Fold down the wings
to the bottom fold.

**5.**

Bring the wings up to
flying position.

Give Plain Plane a big
throw and watch it go!

# Zoom-A-Room

**1.**

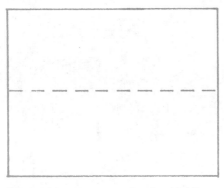

Fold the paper in half like this.

**2.**

Open the paper flat again.

Fold down the corners to the center crease.

**3.**

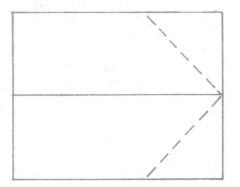

Fold the paper in half again.

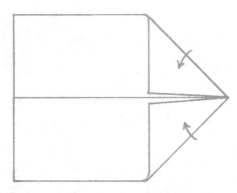

Fold down the corners like this. (Follow the dotted line.)

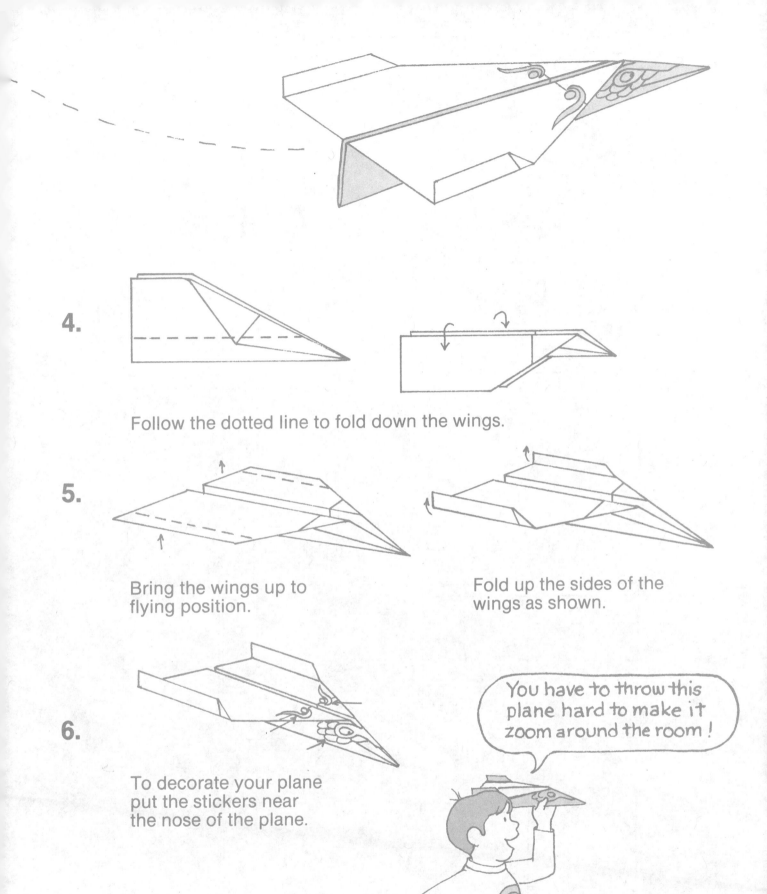

**4.**

Follow the dotted line to fold down the wings.

**5.**

Bring the wings up to flying position.

Fold up the sides of the wings as shown.

**6.**

To decorate your plane put the stickers near the nose of the plane.

You have to throw this plane hard to make it zoom around the room!

# E-Z Flyer

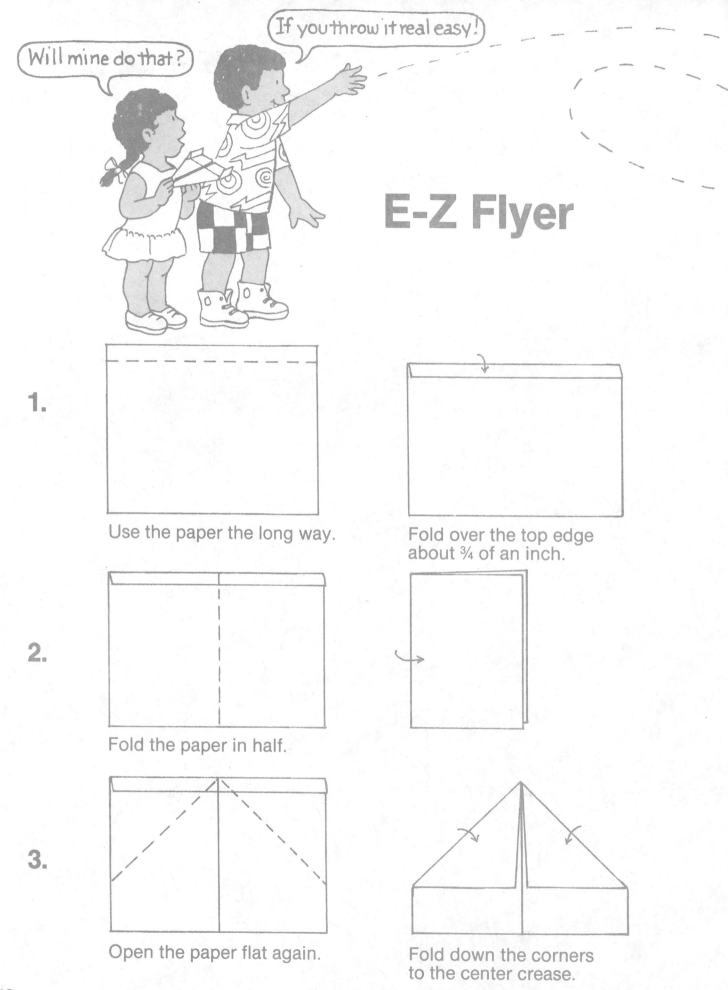

**1.** Use the paper the long way.

Fold over the top edge about ¾ of an inch.

**2.** Fold the paper in half.

**3.** Open the paper flat again.

Fold down the corners to the center crease.

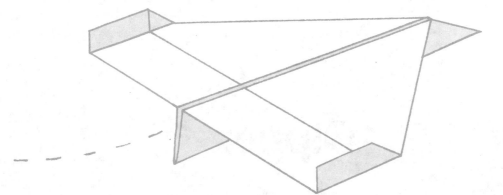

**4.**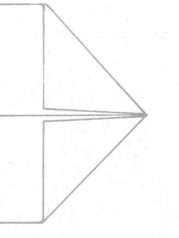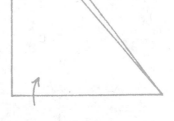

Turn the plane around like this.

Now fold it in half.

**5.**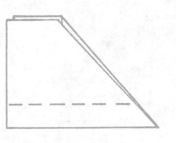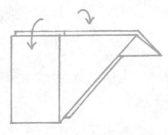

Follow the dotted line to fold down the wings.

**6.**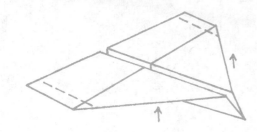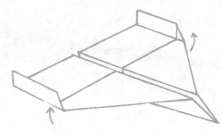

Bring the wings up to flying position.

Fold up the wing tips. Now wasn't that E-Z?

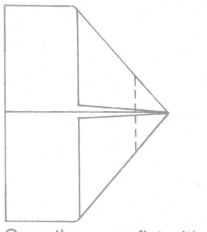

# Dipper

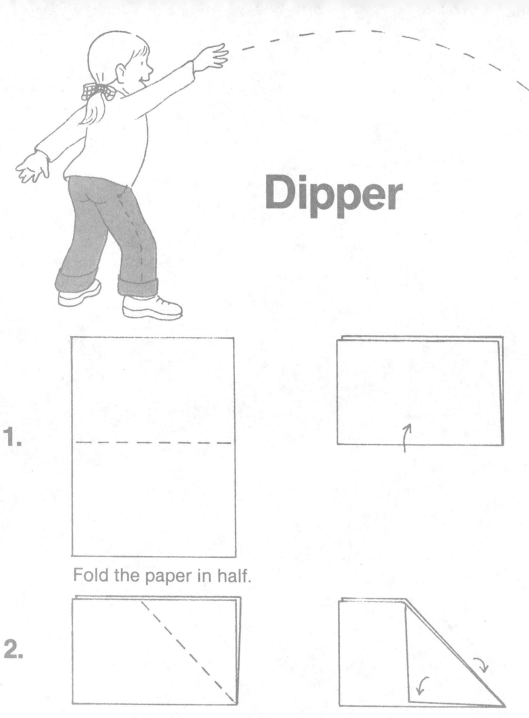

**1.** Fold the paper in half.

**2.** Fold down the corners to the center fold like this.

**3.** Open the paper flat with the folded corners facing you.

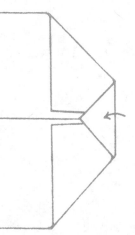

Fold over the pointed end like this.

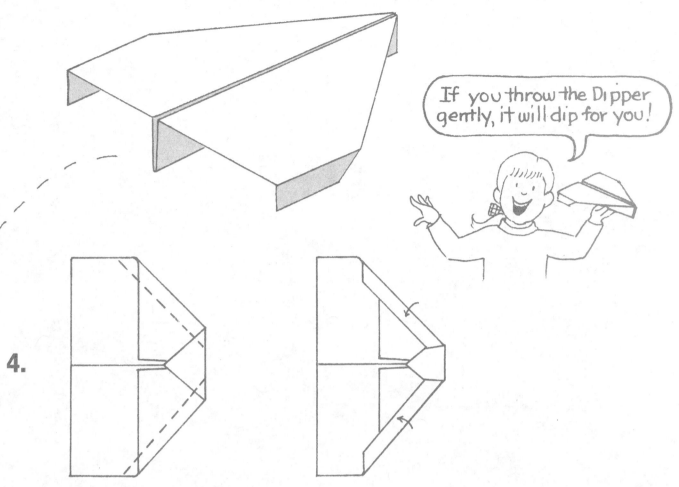

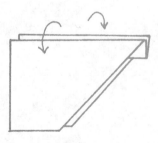

If you throw the Dipper gently, it will dip for you!

**4.**

Fold down the slanted sides like this. (Follow the dotted lines.)

**5.**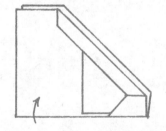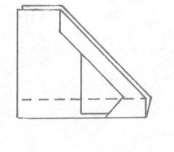

Fold the plane in half so the folded parts are on the outside of the plane.

Follow the dotted line to fold down the wings.

**6.**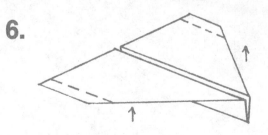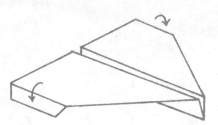

Bring the wings up to flying position.

Fold down the wing tips.

# Shorty

**1.**

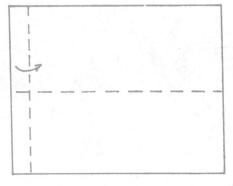

Fold over the end one inch.

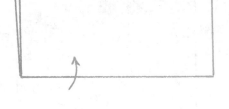

Then fold the paper in half.

**2.**

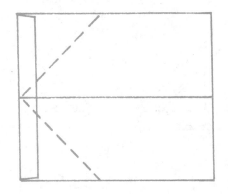

Open the paper flat again.

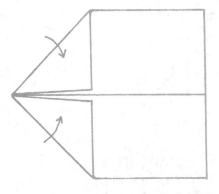

Fold down the corners to the center crease.

**3.**

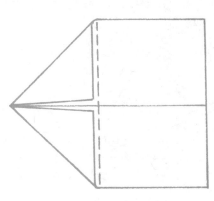

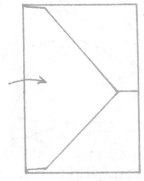

Fold over the pointed end almost to the opposite side.

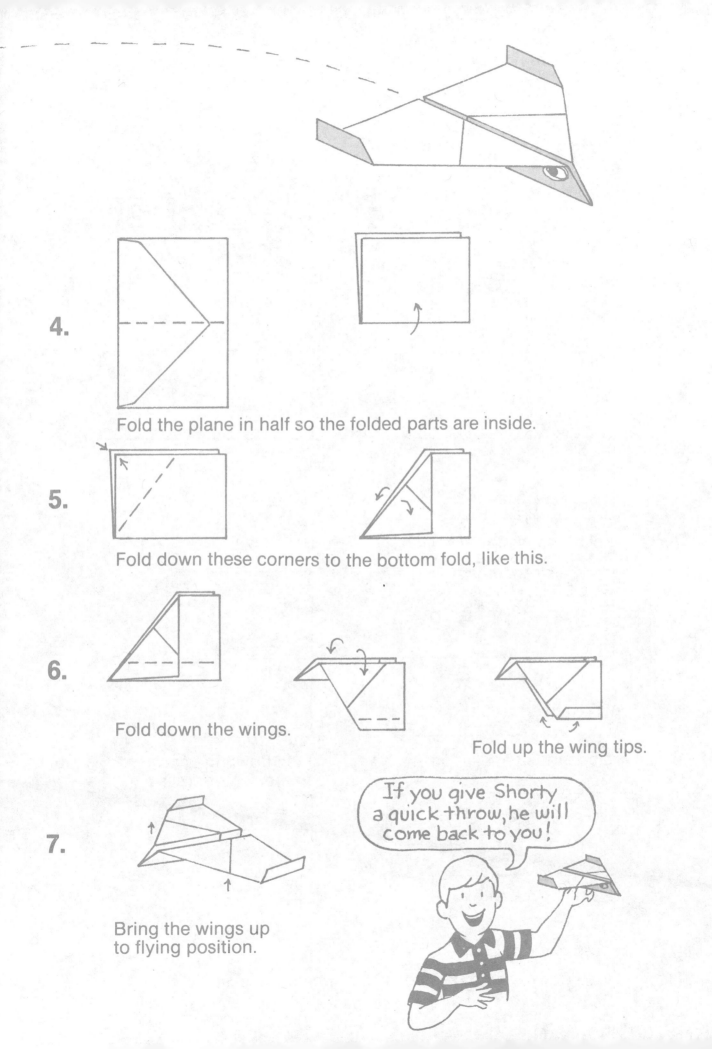

**4.** Fold the plane in half so the folded parts are inside.

**5.** Fold down these corners to the bottom fold, like this.

**6.** Fold down the wings.

Fold up the wing tips.

**7.** Bring the wings up to flying position.

If you give Shorty a quick throw, he will come back to you!

# Dive Bomber

**1.**

Fold the paper in half like this.

**2.**

Open the paper flat again.

Fold down the corners to the center crease.

**3.**

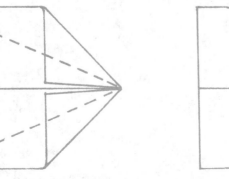

Fold down the corners again to the center crease.

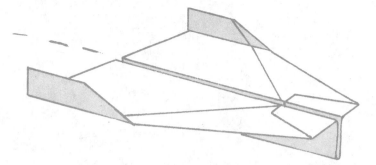

**4.**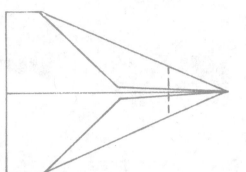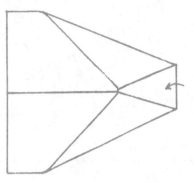

Fold over the pointed end of the plane like this.

**5.**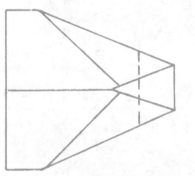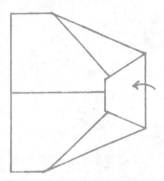

Fold over the end again. Crease the folds well.

**6.**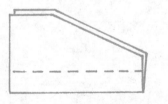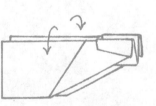

Fold the plane in half.
Follow the dotted line to fold down the wings.

**7.**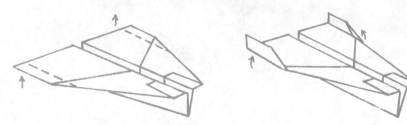

Bring the wings up to flying position.
Fold up the wing tips.

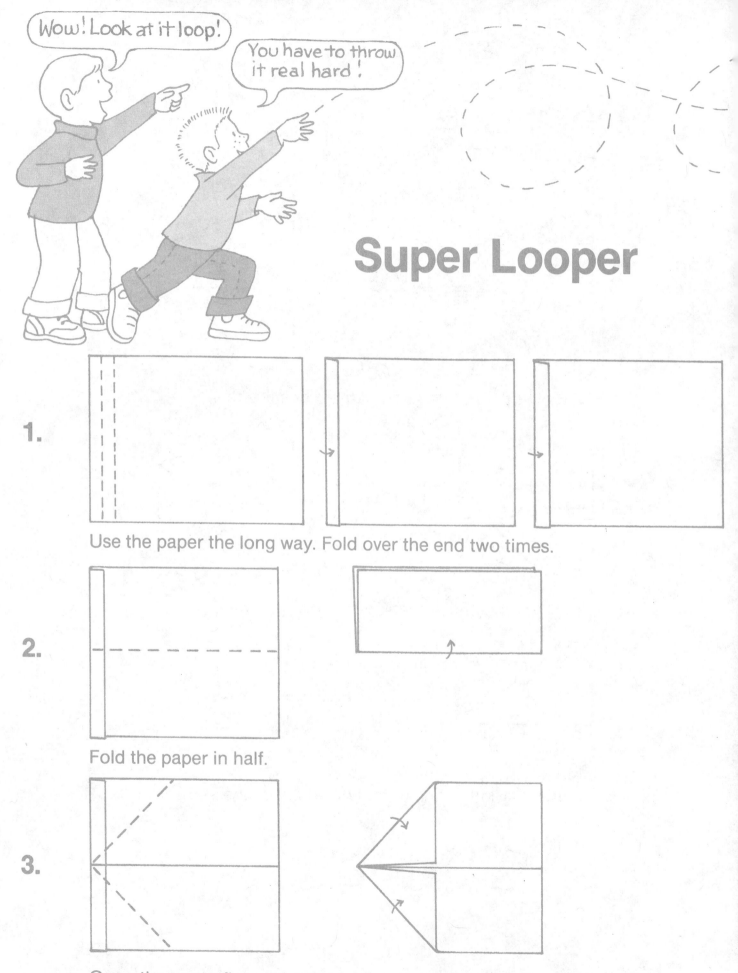

# Super Looper

**1.** Use the paper the long way. Fold over the end two times.

**2.** Fold the paper in half.

**3.** Open the paper flat again. Fold down the corners to the center crease.

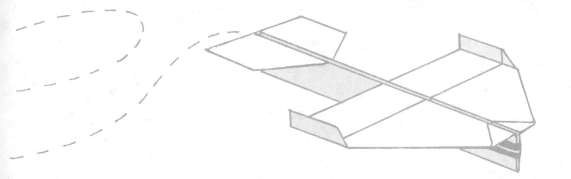

**4.**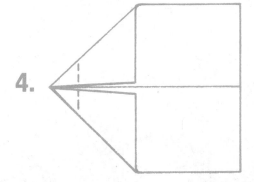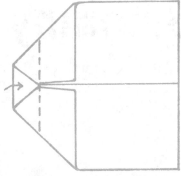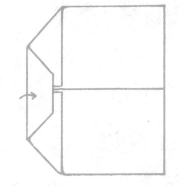

Fold over the pointed end.　　Fold over the end again like this.

**5.**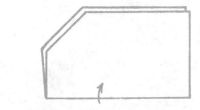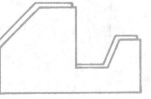

　　Fold the plane in half.　　Cut out (or tear out) a piece of the plane so it looks like this.　(If you do use scissors, make sure a grown-up says it's okay.)

**6.**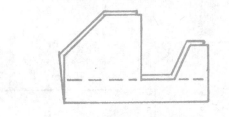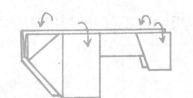

Follow the dotted line to fold down the wings and tail pieces.

**7.**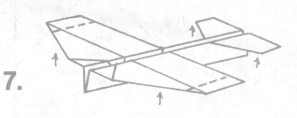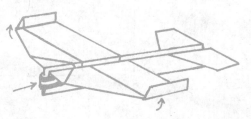

Bring the wings and tail up to flying position.　Fold up the wing tips. Put a sticker around the nose to add weight and hold the body together.

That's smo-o-oth!

# Smoothy

**1.**

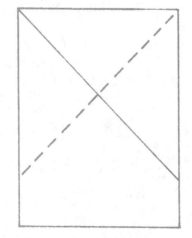

Fold down one corner like this.

**2.**

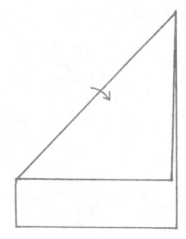

Open the paper flat again.

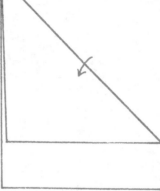

Fold down the other corner.

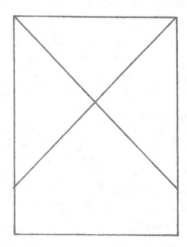

Open the paper flat again. The diagonal creases will look like this.

**3.**

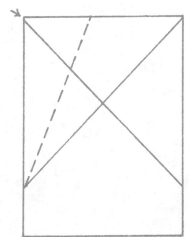 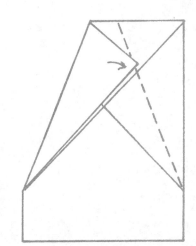 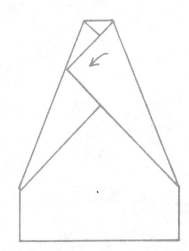

Fold over this corner to the diagonal crease as shown.

Fold over the other corner to the other diagonal crease.

**4.**

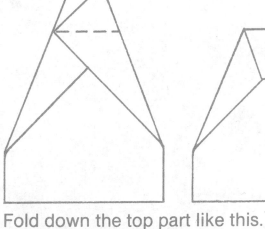 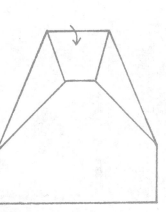 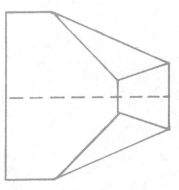

Fold down the top part like this.

Turn the plane around.

**5.**

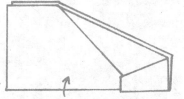

Fold the plane in half with the folded parts on the outside.

Follow the dotted line to fold down the wings.

**6.**

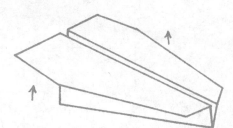

Bring the wings up to flying position.

For the best flight, throw Smoothy gently.

# Little Bat

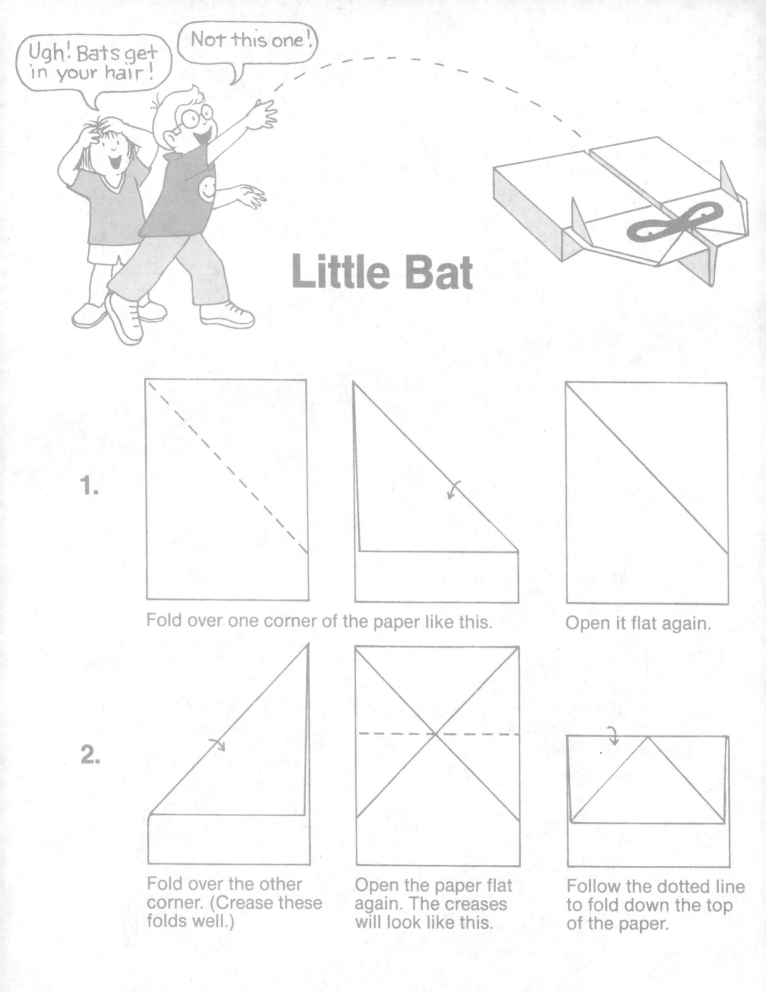

**1.** Fold over one corner of the paper like this.

Open it flat again.

**2.** Fold over the other corner. (Crease these folds well.)

Open the paper flat again. The creases will look like this.

Follow the dotted line to fold down the top of the paper.

**3.**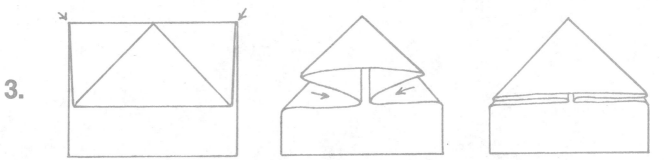

Fold in these two corners iike this. Crease the folds well.

**4.**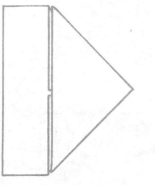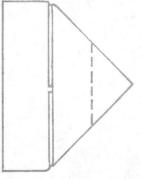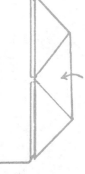

Turn the plane around like this.

Fold over the pointed end like this. Crease the folds well.

**5.**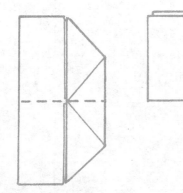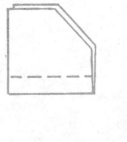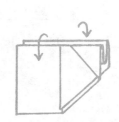

Fold the plane in half with the folded parts inside.

Follow the dotted line to fold down the wings. Crease well. (There will be lots of thicknesses of paper!)

**6.**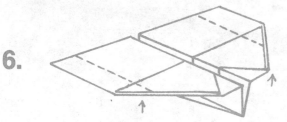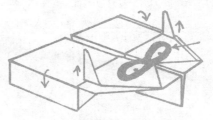

Bring the wings up to flying position.

Fold up the bat's "ears." Fold down the wing tips. Use the bat eyes sticker to decorate and to hold the body together.

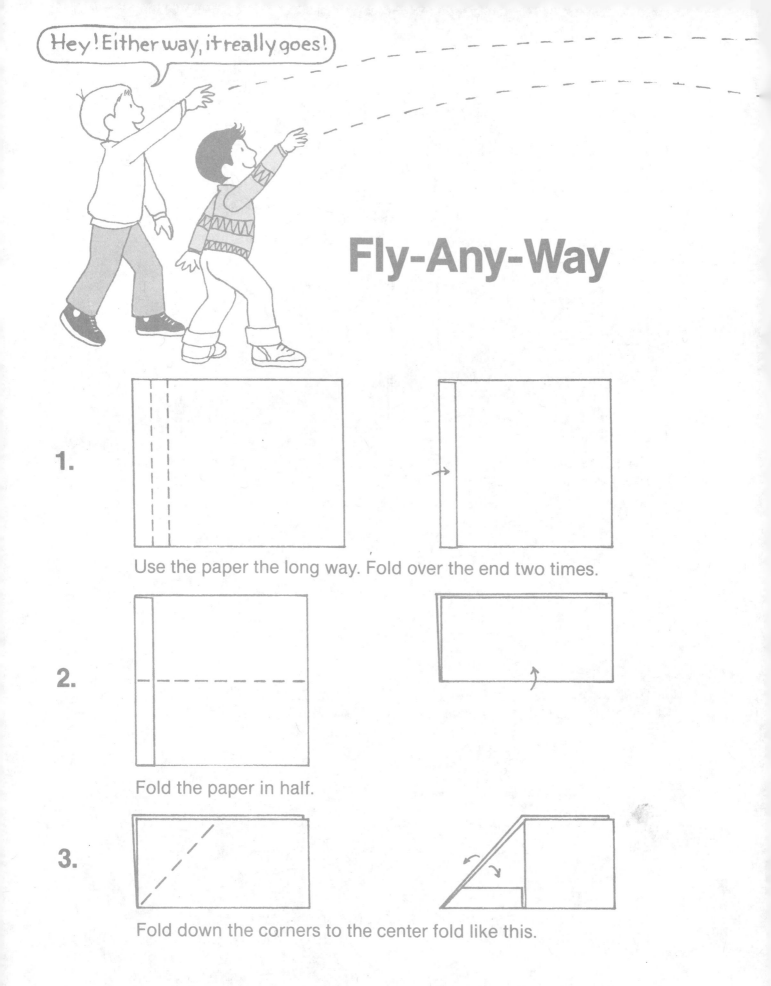

# Fly-Any-Way

**1.** Use the paper the long way. Fold over the end two times.

**2.** Fold the paper in half.

**3.** Fold down the corners to the center fold like this.

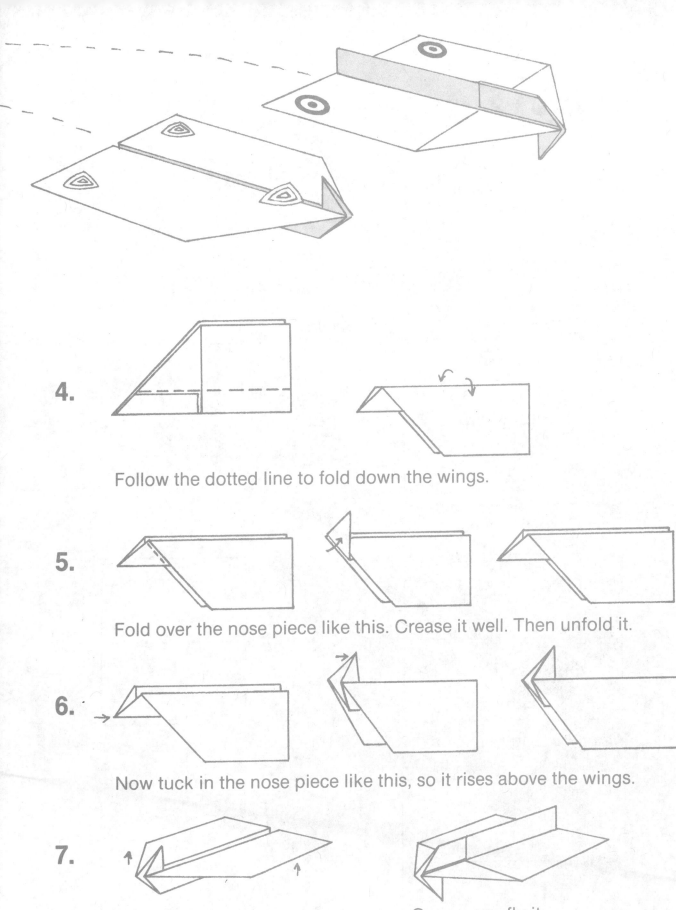

**4.** Follow the dotted line to fold down the wings.

**5.** Fold over the nose piece like this. Crease it well. Then unfold it.

**6.** Now tuck in the nose piece like this, so it rises above the wings.

**7.** Bring the wings up to flying position. You can fly this plane with this side up.

Or you can fly it with this side up. Fly it either way!

# Shooting Star

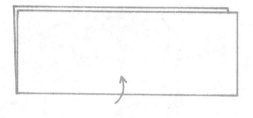

**1.** Fold the paper in half.

**2.** 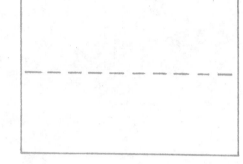 Open the paper flat again.

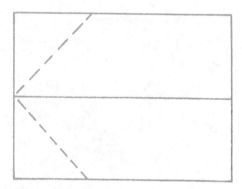 Fold down the corners to the center fold.

**3.** 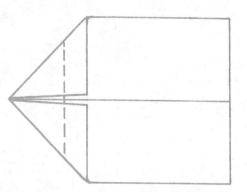 Fold over the pointed end like this.

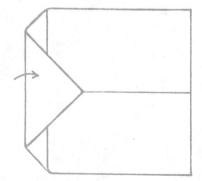

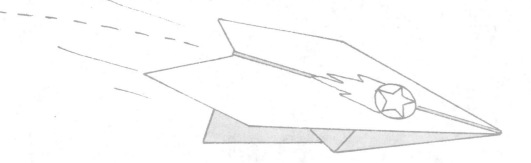

**4.**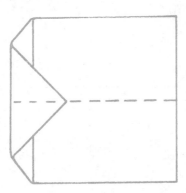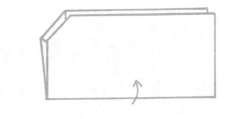

Fold the plane in half with the folded parts inside.

**5.**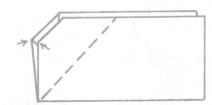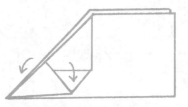

Fold down the corners to the center fold like this.

**6.**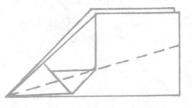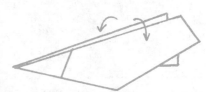

Follow the dotted line to fold down the wings.
Crease the folds well.

**7.**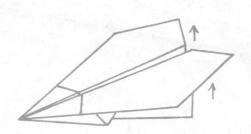

I put the big shooting star sticker right here on my plane. It looks great and goes great!

Bring the wings up to flying position.

# Owl

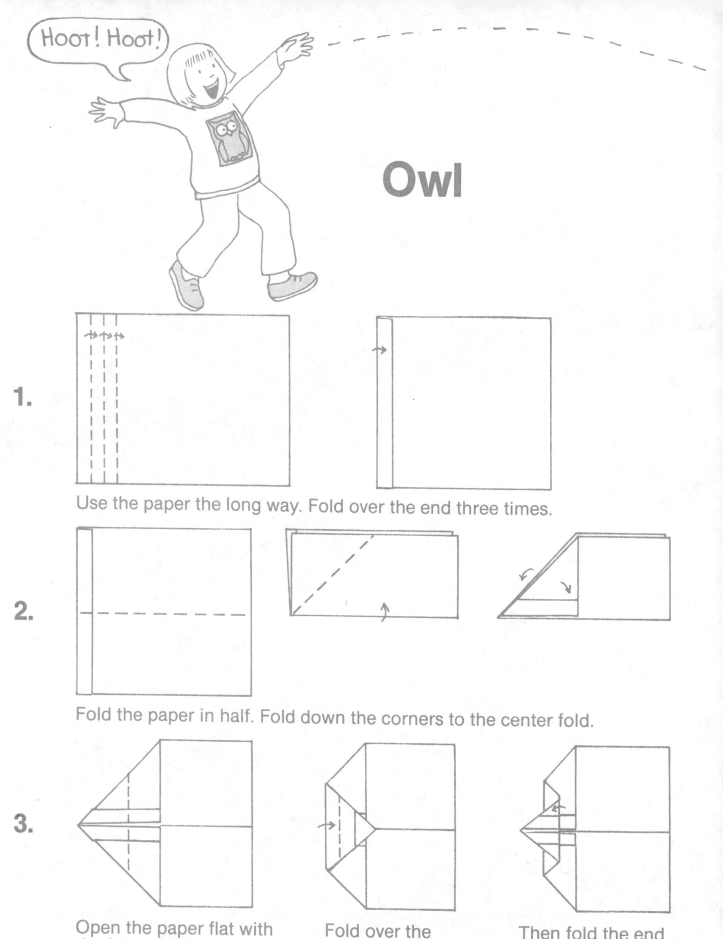

**1.** Use the paper the long way. Fold over the end three times.

**2.** Fold the paper in half. Fold down the corners to the center fold.

**3.** Open the paper flat with the folded corners facing you.

Fold over the pointed end like this.

Then fold the end back like this. Crease the folds well.

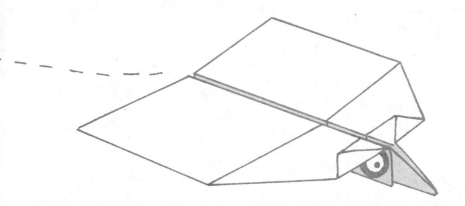

**4.**
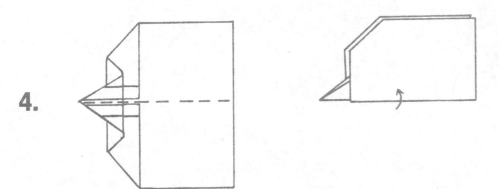

Fold the plane in half with the folded parts inside.

**5.**
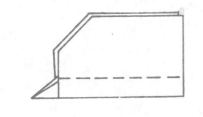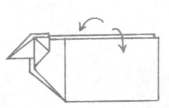

Follow the dotted line to fold down the wings. Crease well.

**6.**
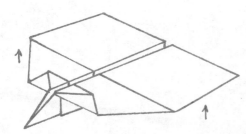

Bring the wings up to flying position.

I used the big yellow eye stickers to make him look like a real owl!

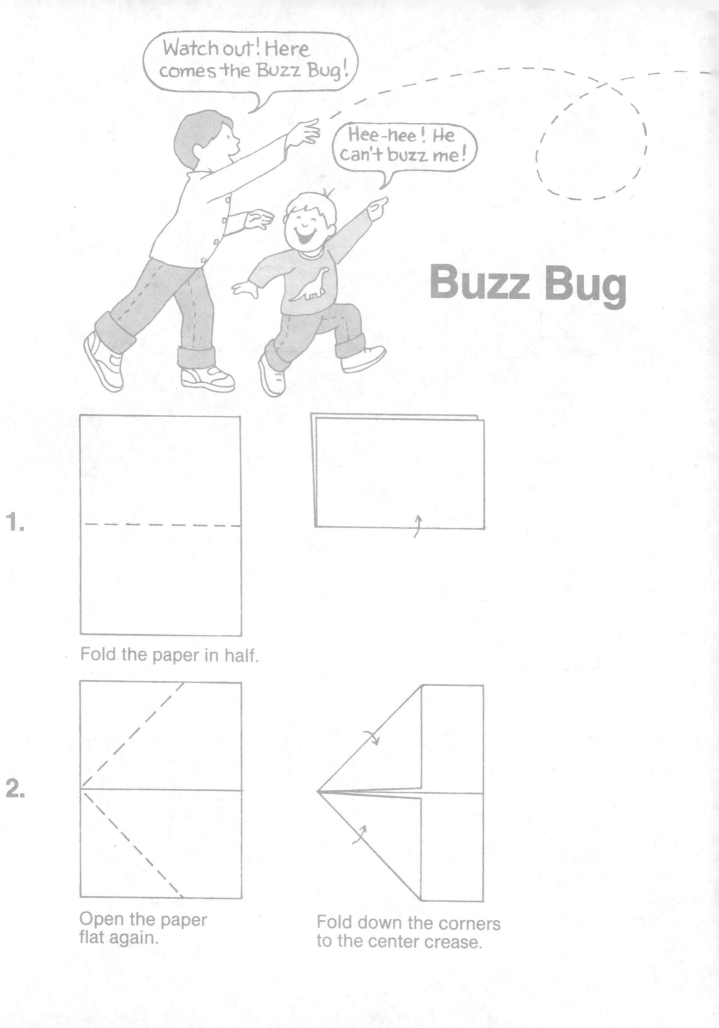

# Buzz Bug

**1.** Fold the paper in half.

**2.** Open the paper flat again.

Fold down the corners to the center crease.

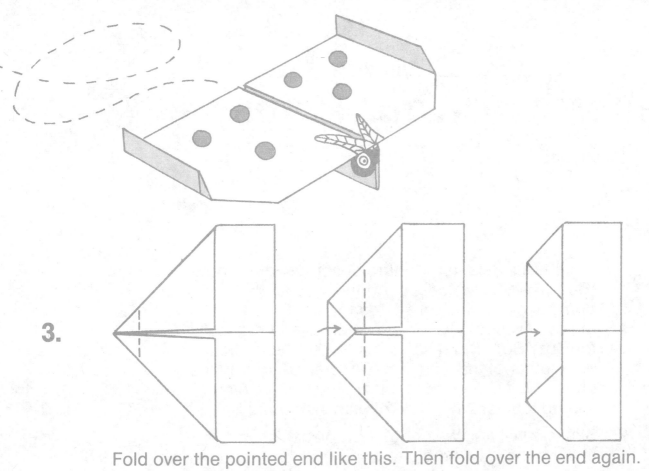

**3.** Fold over the pointed end like this. Then fold over the end again.

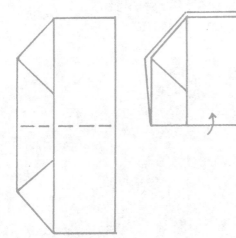

**4.** Fold the plane in half with the folded parts on the outside.

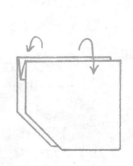

Follow the dotted line to fold down the wings.

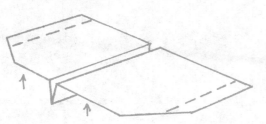

**5.** Bring the wings up to flying position.

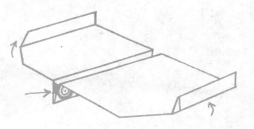

Fold up the wing tips.
Put the big black bug eyes sticker around the nose of the plane.

# Decorating Your Plane

Lazy Drifter

1.  Use the stickers in this kit to decorate your planes. (Be sure you always peel off the stickers carefully!) Some stickers were designed for special planes, like the owl eyes for Owl or the antenna and bug eyes for Buzz Bug. But if you want to use these stickers on another plane, you can. Decorating your plane is up to you—it depends on how you think a plane should look or what type of plane it should be.

2.  Stickers will add weight to your plane. They can change the way the plane will fly. So be very careful where you put the stickers. However, if your plane has lots of weight in its nose, you can put the stickers anywhere on the plane.

3.  You can draw decorations on your plane with crayons or colored pencils or markers. These decorations will not add weight to the plane, so they will not change the way it flies.

4.  Remember, if you use markers to decorate your plane, the marker will come through the paper to the other side! So be sure you want the same decorations on both sides before you start using your markers.

5.  Do not use watercolors to paint your planes. Watercolors will crinkle the paper and your plane will not fly.